< FOUR GREAT AMERICANS >

FOUR GREAT AMERICANS

TRIBUTES DELIVERED BY
PRESIDENT RICHARD NIXON

FOREWORD BY
ADELA ROGERS ST. JOHNS

COMMENTS BY LEE W. HUEBNER
DEPUTY SPECIAL ASSISTANT TO THE PRESIDENT

A Reader's Digest Press Book

DOUBLEDAY & CO., INC.

PHOTO CREDITS:

Pictorial Parade; National Republican Senatorial Committee;
United Press International; Karsh Ottawa

CONTENTS

[*The comments by Lee W. Huebner follow each eulogy*]

FOREWORD

CONTINUE. That is what these tributes, paid by the President of the United States to four great Americans, are really all about.

We need great Americans these days. Let us *continue* those we have had so that we have them still.

In each of these eulogies, paid at a moment when it would seem their work was ended, is the request, the urgent plea, of the President that we continue their words, works, ideals and characters. The excitement rises in our own hearts because their hearts can continue to beat as the only memorial Richard Nixon is willing to accept—that we continue what they have begun.

He tells us clearly about the dream of Whitney Young, imaginative, forceful leader of the Urban League, and then he says, "To fulfill his dream is the responsibility of each of us." Our commitment—to *continue*.

Continue ye in my love—the great Teacher in whom all these men believed said this to us.

We shall continue to remember Everett Dirksen, the President tells us, and then he gives a definition of a politician

< *Foreword* >

which it is my hope will become part of the education of every young American. The word has been allowed to fall into dangerous disrepute and the President rescues it with the finest and most practical definition you have heard and using Senator Dirksen as an example insures he will continue as the *best*.

A deep friendship existed between Richard M. Nixon and J. Edgar Hoover. To their work together when Richard Nixon was a young Congressman their country owes much. Here the President of the United States gives the Director of the FBI a new title, taken from an old one. In the days of the American frontier, he says, the brave men who wore the badge and enforced the law were called peace officers. Without peace officers, the President says, we cannot have peace and J. Edgar Hoover was the peace officer without peer. Let us then, he tells us, honor him by honoring all the men and women who carry on this noble profession of helping to keep peace in our society.

Perhaps not even his own family knew our beloved Dwight D. Eisenhower as did the man who spoke in his honor. No bond could be closer than the one which existed between Richard Nixon and President Eisenhower during the illness that once made it impossible for him to carry on his duties as President. Vice President Nixon responded to his need then with unassuming devotion, carried out his wishes and his orders and gave him the saving peace of knowing that they were being carried out as he wished them to be. You had only to see these two men together, as I did, to recognize how strong was the love between them. Here the man who is now President says, "This man who led the most

< *Foreword* >

powerful armies that the world has ever seen, this man who led the most powerful nation in the world, this essentially good and gentle and kind man, whose Bible was his daily guide, had his true greatness in moral force."

Four very different men, it seems. Eisenhower, Young, Dirksen and Hoover. Yet as he spoke of these men at different times, in different places, Richard Nixon found their point of shared strength.

As a man thinketh in his *heart* so is he.

Above all their talents, achievements, fame and power you will find is the heart he presents in all of them. They came from the heart of America, spoke to the heart of America, and when a man speaks to and with and for and of the heart of America, all things will be well.

In the pages that follow, the President of the United States, himself a man of great heart, shares with us the words he spoke about these great men who should continue forever in our memory.

ADELA ROGERS ST. JOHNS

< FOUR GREAT AMERICANS >

EULOGY

Mrs. EISENHOWER, Your Excellencies, friends of Dwight David Eisenhower in America and throughout the world:

We gather today in mourning, but also in gratitude.

We mourn Dwight Eisenhower's death, but we are grateful for his life.

We gather, also, conscious of the fact that in paying tribute to Dwight Eisenhower, we celebrate greatness. When we think of his place in history, we think, inevitably, of the other giants of those days of World War II; and we think of the qualities of greatness and what his were that made his unique among all.

Once, perhaps without intending to do so, he himself put his finger on it. It was 1945, shortly after V-E Day, at a ceremony in London's historic Guildhall. The triumphant Supreme Commander of the Allied

13

< *Four Great Americans* >

Forces in Europe was officially given the Freedom of the City of London.

In an eloquent address that day, Dwight Eisenhower said: "I come from the heart of America."

Perhaps no one sentence could better sum up what Dwight Eisenhower meant to a whole generation of Americans. He did come from the heart of America, not only from its geographical heart, but from its spiritual heart.

He exemplified what millions of parents hoped that their sons would be: strong and courageous and honest and compassionate. And with his own great qualities of heart, he personified the best in America.

It is, I think, a special tribute to Dwight Eisenhower that despite all of his honors, despite all of his great deeds and his triumphs, we find ourselves today thinking, first, not of his deeds but of his character. It was the character of the man, not what he did but what he was, that so captured the trust and faith and affection of his own people and of the people of the world.

Dwight Eisenhower touched something fundamental in America which only a man of immense force of mind and spirit could have brought so vibrantly alive. He was a product of America's soil and of its ideals, driven by a compulsion to do right and to do well; a

< *Dwight Eisenhower* >

man of deep faith who believed in God and trusted in His will; a man who truly loved his country and for whom words like "freedom" and "democracy" were not clichés, but they were living truths.

I know Mrs. Eisenhower would permit me to share with you the last words he spoke to her on the day he died. He said: "I have always loved my wife. I have always loved my children. I have always loved my grandchildren. And I have always loved my country." That was Dwight Eisenhower.

He was a man who gave enormously of himself. His way of relaxing from the intense pressures of office or command was to do something else intensely, whether as a fierce competitor on the golf course or executing one of those hauntingly beautiful paintings that he did with such meticulous care. But even more than this, he gave enormously of himself to people. People loved Dwight Eisenhower. But the other side of this coin was that he loved people.

He had the great leader's capacity to bring out the best in people. He had the great humanist's capacity to inspire people, to cheer them, to give them lift.

I remember, for example, just a few months ago when I asked all of the members of the Cabinet to go out and call on him. And each of them returned with

< *Four Great Americans* >

wonder and admiration and said: "You know, I went out there to cheer him up and instead I found he cheered me up."

His great love of people was rooted in his faith. He had a deep faith in the goodness of God and in the essential goodness of man as a creature of God.

This feeling toward people had another side. In the political world, strong passions are the norm and all too often these turn toward personal vindictiveness. People often disagreed with Dwight Eisenhower, but almost nobody ever hated him. And this, I think, was because he himself was a man who did not know how to hate.

Oh, he could be aroused by a cause, but he could not hate a person. He could disagree strongly, even passionately, but never personally.

When people disagreed with him, he never thought of them as enemies. He simply thought: "Well, they don't agree with me."

I remember time after time, when critics of one sort or another were misrepresenting him or reviling him, he would sit back in his chair and with that wonderful half smile and half frown, he would say: "I am puzzled by those fellows." And he was genuinely puzzled by frenzy and by hate. Because he was incapable of it

16

< Dwight Eisenhower >

himself, he could never quite understand it in others.

The last time I saw him that was what he talked about. He was puzzled by the hatreds he had seen in our times. And he said the thing the world needs most today is understanding, an ability to see the other person's point of view and not to hate him because he disagrees.

That was Dwight Eisenhower.

And yet, of course, he was more than all that. He had a side more evident to those of us who worked with him than to the rest of the world. He was a strong man. He was shrewd. He was decisive.

Time and again I have seen him make decisions that probably made the difference between war and peace for America and the world.

That was always when he was at his best. No matter how heated the arguments were, he was always then the coolest man in the room.

Dwight Eisenhower was that rarest of men, an authentic hero.

Wars bring the names of many men into the headlines and of those some few become national or even international heroes. But as the years then pass, their fame goes down.

But not so with Dwight Eisenhower. As the years

< *Four Great Americans* >

passed, his stature grew: Commander of the mightiest expeditionary force ever assembled, receiver of the surrender of the German Armies in World War II, president of Columbia University, Supreme Commander of NATO, thirty-fourth President of the United States. The honors, the offices were there in abundance. Every trust that the American people had it in their power to bestow, he was given.

And, yet, he always retained a saving humility. His was the humility not of fear but of confidence. He walked with the great of the world, and he knew that the great are human. His was the humility of man before God and before the truth. His was the humility of a man too proud to be arrogant.

The pursuit of peace was uppermost in his mind when he ran for the presidency. And it was uppermost in his conduct of that office. And it is a tribute to his skill and determination that not since the 1930s has the nation enjoyed so long a period of peace, both at home and abroad, as the one that began in 1953 and continued through his presidency.

As Commander of the mightiest allied force ever assembled, he was the right man at the right place at the right time. And as President, once again he was the right man at the right place at the right time.

18

< Dwight Eisenhower >

He restored calm to a divided nation. He gave Americans a new measure of self-respect. He invested his office with dignity and respect and trust. He made Americans proud of their President, proud of their country, proud of themselves. And if we in America were proud of Dwight Eisenhower, it was partly because he made us proud of America.

He came from the heart of America. And he gave expression to the heart of America, and he touched the hearts of the world.

Many leaders are known and respected outside their own countries. Very few are loved outside their own countries. Dwight Eisenhower was one of those few. He was probably loved by more people in more parts of the world than any President America has ever had.

He captured the deepest feelings of free men everywhere. The principles he believed in, the ideals he stood for, these were bigger than his own country.

Perhaps he himself put it best again in that Guildhall speech in 1945. He said then: "Kinship among nations is not determined in such measurements as proximity, size and age. Rather, we should turn to those inner things—call them what you will—I mean those intangibles that are the real treasures free men possess.

"To preserve his freedom of worship, his equality

< *Four Great Americans* >

before law, his liberty to speak and act as he sees fit, subject only to provisions that he trespass not upon similar rights of others—a Londoner will fight. So will a citizen of Abilene. When we consider these things, then the valley of the Thames draws closer to the farms of Kansas and the plains of Texas."

Some men are considered great because they lead great armies or they lead powerful nations. For eight years now, Dwight Eisenhower has neither commanded an army nor led a nation. And, yet, he remained through his final days the world's most admired and respected man—truly, the first citizen of the world.

As we marvel at this, it leads us once again to ponder the mysteries of greatness. Dwight Eisenhower's greatness derived not from his office, but from his character, from a unique moral force that transcended national boundaries, even as his own deep concern for humanity transcended national boundaries.

His life reminds us that there is a moral force in this world more powerful than the might of arms or the wealth of nations. This man who led the most powerful armies that the world has ever seen, this man who led the most powerful nation in the world, this essentially good and gentle and kind man—that moral force was his greatness.

< Dwight Eisenhower >

For a quarter of a century to the very end of his life Dwight Eisenhower exercised a moral authority without parallel in America and in the world. And America and the world are better because of it.

And so today we render our final salute. It is a fond salute to a man we loved and cherished. It is a grateful salute to a man whose whole extraordinary life was consecrated to service. It is a profoundly respectful salute to a man larger than life who by any standard was one of the giants of our time.

Each of us here will have a special memory of Dwight Eisenhower. I can see him now standing erect, straight, proud and tall sixteen years ago as he took the oath of office as the thirty-fourth President of the United States of America.

We salute Dwight David Eisenhower standing there in our memories, first in war, first in peace, and, wherever freedom is cherished, first in the hearts of his fellow men.

———

IT was shortly after V-E Day in 1945 that Lieutenant Commander Richard Nixon, standing at a twentieth-story window in downtown New York, first saw General of the Army Dwight David Eisenhower. The returning war hero was riding triumphantly through a blizzard of ticker tape, his arms stretched high above him in his famous victory salute. Seven years later, Senator Richard Nixon of California stood at the side of the General in Chicago as he greeted the Republican National Convention with the same salute and accepted its presidential nomination.

Nixon remained at Eisenhower's side for the next eight years, charged with greater responsibilities than those of any previous Vice President. When Nixon was narrowly defeated in his own bid for the presidency in 1960, Eisenhower said he felt as though he "had been hit in the solar plexus with a ball bat." Nixon's defeat, he wrote later, had been his "principal political disappointment."

Seven years after leaving the White House, in April of 1968, General Eisenhower suffered a heart attack while on a golfing vacation in California. He was flown to Washington and entered Walter Reed Army Medical Center where he spent the last ten months of his life in a three-room suite on the top floor of the Walter Reed's east wing. From there he issued a pre-Convention endorsement of Nixon's second bid for the presidency and from there he addressed the Republican National Convention in August. As he battled courageously against recurrent heart problems in the late summer and fall, he said that his ambition now was to live to greet two events: the marriage of his grandson David to Julie Nixon in December and the Inauguration of Richard Nixon in January.

Both wishes were fulfilled.

One month after the Inauguration, on February 23, 1969, the General underwent abdominal surgery. On February 28, he contracted the flu but fought back courageously—as he

< Dwight Eisenhower >

had in overcoming seven heart attacks. On March 15, however, he developed congestive heart failure and for the next two weeks his wife, Mamie, staying in an adjoining two-room suite, told friends that she lived only "from day to day." When President Nixon came to visit his old chief on March 26, the General gathered his waning energies, flashed his famous grin, reached out his hand and said, "Hi, Mr. President!" (The day before Mr. Nixon's Inauguration, General Eisenhower had telephoned him, and said that he wanted to use that last opportunity to say, "Hi, Dick"—that from then on he would always call him "Mr. President.")

On that visit—as he always does when visiting a person in a hospital—President Nixon made a point of not talking about the General's illness, but rather of seeking his advice about the problems of the nation and the world. The President had just returned from a trip to Europe; he reviewed the trip and passed along a number of messages for General Eisenhower from European leaders he had met with. The two Presidents exchanged a long series of personal recollections about one of those leaders—President de Gaulle of France.

That visit on March 26 was their last together.

At 4 A.M. on Friday, March 28, the General began to slip badly, though he remained generally alert through the morning. With him in his final hours were Mamie, his son, John, and David and Julie Eisenhower, who had flown in from a Florida vacation a day earlier. When the end came at 12:25 P.M., Julie telephoned her father at the White House. The President had been told of the General's death just moments before by his personal physician, Dr. Walter R. Tkach, who had been eating lunch at the White House mess when he was

< *Four Great Americans* >

informed of Eisenhower's death by Colonel John Bradley, executive officer at the Walter Reed Hospital.

The President had just finished a meeting of the National Security Council, and was talking in the Oval Office with Secretary of Defense Melvin Laird and presidential assistants H. R. Haldeman and Henry Kissinger when Tkach brought the news. The President had been waiting to speak by phone with Archbishop Terence Cooke of New York, who, it had just been announced, was to be elevated to the College of Cardinals. Cooke was at a Washington meeting of the National Commission on the Causes and Prevention of Violence. As he went to the phone, Cooke noticed the Chairman of the Commission, Dr. Milton Eisenhower, standing at a phone next to him with tears running down his face. When the President's call to Cooke was canceled, the Archbishop immediately knew the reason.

After taking Julie's call, the President called Mrs. Nixon, who was in the residence area of the White House, and a few minutes later she and Tricia Nixon joined the President in a motorcade to the hospital, along with Laird, Haldeman, Kissinger, Secretary of State William Rogers and presidential assistant Bryce Harlow—who had served Eisenhower in the White House and had been close to him in his post-presidential years. They were greeted at the door by Mrs. Eisenhower, who took them into the General's room, where his body still lay. Milton Eisenhower arrived shortly afterward. The group spent twenty-five minutes in quiet conversation. The Nixons then returned to the White House, and shortly before 4 P.M. the President left by helicopter for Camp David, the Maryland mountain retreat which Eisenhower had renamed in

< Dwight Eisenhower >

honor of his grandson. There the President prepared his thoughts for the Sunday afternoon eulogy which the General had asked that he deliver.

The eulogy presented President Nixon with a unique responsibility, for he wanted to speak both officially and personally on this solemn occasion. As the nation's President, he wanted to voice its collective sentiments for a former President and fallen hero. As a personal friend, he wanted to express his own individual feelings for a man who had been his mentor and supporter. He knew that whatever he said had to come both from his heart and from his office.

As he pondered the assignment, the President decided to write the speech as Eisenhower would have written it—with simplicity and with dignity, focusing not on events and deeds or the trappings of a great career but rather on the person, on the qualities of character which Eisenhower valued so much more than decorations and honors. This focus was evident in the three brief documents issued by the President immediately following Eisenhower's death on Friday afternoon: a formal announcement to the Congress, a proclamation declaring a period of national mourning and a personal statement; in all three he expressed thoughts which would later appear in his eulogy. In the proclamation, for example, he quoted from the General's 1945 speech at London's historic Guildhall, a favorite document which Nixon had cited on many previous occasions, including his own Guildhall speech in 1958, and which he would quote from again at two points in the eulogy.

As the President flew to Camp David and as he rested there (fighting a bad cold and even working on the speech in bed from time to time) he recalled his own last impressions of

Eisenhower, those of his Cabinet members and those of the General's family, including Mamie's moving report of his last words to her—which the President decided he should share with the nation on Sunday. He was struck again by Eisenhower's continuing emphasis, even in his last days, on the young people of the country, his faith in their idealism and his distress at the rancor which seemed to plague so many college campuses. The subject was one which was also very much on President Nixon's mind during these days. Reports already were coming to him about the trouble which was expected on campuses in the spring. He had campaigned on a pledge to bring the country together; in his Inaugural Address he had called upon Americans to "lower our voices." As he thought about the General's life, he naturally focused on those qualities which made him the great conciliator, the symbol of national unity.

"Everybody loved him," the President reflected to an aide, "and the reason was that he loved everybody. He was genuinely puzzled by personal hostility. He just could not conceive of anybody really hating another person, no matter what their disagreements.

"I never called him Ike," the President went on, as he remembered the overpowering dignity of the man. And yet the General was also a very humble person. Perhaps in his speech the President could comment on the relationship of pride and humility in the Eisenhower character. And certainly, speaking for the nation, he wanted to comment on what Eisenhower meant to the entire world.

The President returned to the White House at 1:45 P.M. on Sunday. In the late afternoon he left for Washington's Na-

tional Cathedral where, in accordance with a fifty-four-page
funeral plan which had been approved by General Eisenhower
in 1966, his body had been lying in state since Saturday noon.
A solemn military funeral procession with muffled drums and
the traditional riderless horse escorted the body from the
Cathedral to the Capitol. It was a cold, gray day, but as the
cortege approached the Capitol at 4:25 the sun broke through
the overcast. The $80 military-issue coffin, draped with the
American flag, was carried to its place of honor in the center
of the Rotunda—resting there on the same catafalque which
had borne the body of Lincoln and six subsequent Presidents
and twelve national heroes. Here, flanked by the Eisenhower
and Nixon families, the Congress, the Supreme Court, the
Cabinet, the diplomatic corps and other dignitaries—and
joined by millions of Americans through television and radio
—the President delivered his eulogy.

Even as the ceremony proceeded, the lines of visitors began
to stretch across the Capitol Plaza and beyond the Supreme
Court Building two blocks away. Throughout Sunday night
and Monday morning they would walk past the coffin in
silent tribute—as they had done at the National Cathedral.
On Monday afternoon General Eisenhower's body would be
returned to the Cathedral for the state funeral service, attended by national leaders from all over the world. From
there, it would move by special funeral train to the plains of
Kansas, where President Nixon would join with mourners at
graveside ceremonies on Wednesday, April 2. And as the
train rolled across the Midwest on March 31, David Eisenhower would mark his twenty-first birthday—on the day of
his grandfather's funeral.   L. W. H.

EULOGY

DELIVERED BY THE PRESIDENT

AT THE CAPITOL ROTUNDA

SEPTEMBER 9, 1969

Mrs. DIRKSEN, Mr. Vice President, Mr. Chief Justice, Members of the Congress, Members of the Cabinet, Members of the Diplomatic Corps, Your Excellencies, and friends of Everett Dirksen throughout the nation:

When Daniel Webster died more than a century ago, a man who differed strongly with him on many public issues rose in Congress to say this in eulogy: "Our great men are the common property of the country."

Everett Dirksen, of Illinois, was and is the "common property" of all the fifty states.

Senator Dirksen belonged to all of us because he always put his country first. He was an outspoken partisan, he was an individualist of the first rank, but he put his nation before himself and before his party.

He came to the nation's capital in 1932, and his public service spanned an era of enormous change in

< *Four Great Americans* >

the life of our country. He played a vital part in that change. That is why it is so difficult to think of the Washington scene, of this Capitol, without him.

Only his fellow legislators, the Senators and Representatives who have gathered here today and who mourn his loss across the nation, know the full extent of his contribution to the process of governing this country.

They know the time and concern he put into their bills, their causes, their problems. They know another side to Everett Dirksen—the side in the committees and behind the scenes where so much of the hard work and the hard bargaining is done, where there is so little that makes headlines and so much that makes legislation.

Through four presidencies, through the adult life of most Americans living today, Everett Dirksen has had a hand in shaping almost every important law that affects our lives.

Everett Dirksen was a politician in the finest sense of that much abused word. If he were here, I think he might put it this way:

A politician knows that more important than the bill that is proposed is the law that is passed.

A politician knows that his friends are not always

< *Everett Dirksen* >

his allies and that his adversaries are not his enemies.

A politician knows how to make the process of democracy work and loves the intricate workings of the democratic system.

A politician knows not only how to count votes, but how to make his vote count.

A politician knows that his words are his weapons, but that his word is his bond.

A politician knows that only if he leaves room for discussion and room for concession can he gain room for maneuver.

A politician knows that the best way to be a winner is to make the other side feel it does not have to be a loser.

And a politician—in the Dirksen tradition—knows both the name of the game and the rules of the game, and he seeks his ends through the time-honored democratic means.

By being that kind of politician, this "Man of the Minority" earned the respect and affection of the majority. And by the special way he gave leadership to legislation, he added grace and elegance and courtliness to the word "politician."

That is how he became the leader of a minority, and one of the leaders of our nation. And that is why, when

< *Four Great Americans* >

the Senate worked its way, Everett Dirksen so often worked his way.

That is why, while he never became President, his impact and influence on the nation was greater than that of most Presidents in our history.

He was at once a tough-minded man and a complete gentleman. He could take issue without taking offense. And if that is an example of the "old politics," let us hope that it always has a place in the politics of the future.

He is a man to be remembered, as we remember the other giants of the Senate—the Websters and Calhouns, the Vandenbergs and the Tafts.

Some will remember his voice—that unforgettable voice—that rolled as deep and majestically as the river that defines the western border of the state of Illinois he loved so well. Others will remember the unfailing— often self-deprecating—sense of humor which proved that a man of serious purpose need never take himself too seriously.

Others will remember the mastery of language, the gift of oratory that placed him in a class with Bryan and Churchill, showing, as only he would put it, that "The oil can is mightier than the sword."

But as we do honor to his memory, let us never for-

< *Everett Dirksen* >

get the single quality that made him unique, the quality that made him powerful, made him beloved: the quality of character.

Everett Dirksen cultivated an appearance that made him seem old-fashioned, an incarnation of a bygone year. But that quality of character is as modern as a Saturn V.

As he could persuade, he could be persuaded. His respect for other points of view lent weight to his own point of view. He was not afraid to change his position if he were persuaded that he had been wrong. That tolerance and sympathy were elements of his character and that character gained him the affection and esteem of millions of his fellow Americans.

We shall always remember Everett Dirksen in the terms he used to describe his beloved marigolds: hardy, vivid, exuberant, colorful—and uniquely American.

To his family, his staff and his legion of friends who knew and loved Everett Dirksen, I would like to add a personal word.

There are memorable moments we will never know again—those eloquent speeches, the incomparable anecdotes, those wonderfully happy birthday parties.

But he, least of all, would want this to be a sad occasion. With his dramatic sense of history, I can

< *Four Great Americans* >

hear him now speaking of the glory of this moment.

As a man of politics, he knew both victory and defeat.

As a student of philosophy, he knew the triumph of and the tragedy and the misery of life.

And as a student of history, he knew that some men achieve greatness; others are not recognized for their greatness until after their death. Only a privileged few live to hear the favorable verdict of history on their careers.

Two thousand years ago the poet Sophocles wrote: "One must wait until the evening to see how splendid the day has been."

We who were privileged to be his friends can take comfort in the fact that Everett Dirksen—in the rich evening of his life, his leadership unchallenged, his mind clear, his great voice still powerful across the land—could look back upon his life and say: The day has indeed been splendid.

———

THE SUMMER of 1969 was an exceptionally eventful period for the new President. He circled the globe in midsummer, welcoming the first men to walk on the moon after their splashdown in the Pacific, enunciating his new Nixon Doctrine in foreign policy, becoming the first President to

< Everett Dirksen >

visit Saigon and, in Bucharest, Rumania, the first to visit the capital of a communist country. He won important legislative battles over the surtax and the ABM and, on August 8, he presented a dramatic program of domestic reforms including welfare, manpower-training and revenue-sharing programs. All this happened in just a sixteen-day period. On August 9 the President flew to his new summer home at San Clemente, California, and there he established for the next month a working Western White House.

It was on the very last day of this California stay, on Sunday afternoon, September 7 at 2:21 P.M. Pacific time, that President Nixon received a phone call at his residence from H. R. Haldeman reporting the sudden death of Everett McKinley Dirksen. The President spoke briefly by phone with Bryce Harlow, then placed a call to Mrs. Dirksen in Washington. The Minority Leader of the Senate had entered Walter Reed Army Medical Center in Washington on August 31 for surgery to remove a malignant tumor from his lung. The President, who had last seen Dirksen at a Republican congressional leadership meeting on August 8, spoke with him by phone from San Clemente on September 1, the day before his scheduled operation. The three-hour operation on September 2 had been successful, the cancer had not spread and doctors expected the Illinois Senator to be out of the hospital in six weeks. Then in midafternoon on September 7 he "sustained a sudden cardiac and respiratory arrest." He died at 4:52 P.M., two hours later. In the President's absence, Vice President Agnew went immediately to the hospital to visit Mrs. Dirksen.

While the burial services would take place in Illinois in the Senator's home town of Pekin, it was promptly decided that

< *Four Great Americans* >

the Senator's body would first lie in state in the Rotunda of the nation's Capitol where he had served for so many years, as a member of the House of Representatives from 1933 to 1949 and as a Senator since 1951. Mrs. Dirksen asked the President to deliver the eulogy at the Capitol, and he promptly agreed to do so.

The President could not retreat to work on his speech as he had after Eisenhower's death. The next day, Monday, September 8, was especially busy, as the presidential party left San Clemente and headed first to the Amistad Dam on the Mexican-American border for dedication ceremonies and talks with the President of Mexico. Next the President's plane headed for the coastal areas of Mississippi which had recently been devastated by Hurricane Camille, landing at Gulfport where the President spoke to an airport crowd about courage in the face of adversity. With the three-hour-time loss, it was late in the evening when Air Force One touched down at Andrews Air Force Base outside Washington. The President worked on his speech during the flight to Washington, then returned to it again after arriving at the White House—where he continued working on it until 3 A.M.

The previous Republican President, Dwight D. Eisenhower, had also lost his Senate Republican Leader, Robert Taft, in the summer of his first year in office. Richard Nixon could remember how significant that loss was for Eisenhower —and wondered what impact Dirksen's death would have on the success of his own emerging legislative program in a Congress controlled by the opposition party. The Minority Leader had recently been a key figure, for example, in the extremely narrow Senate vote to support the ABM.

< Everett Dirksen >

Dirksen's unique skill, ever since Nixon, then a freshman Congressman, first met him in 1947, was his ability to work behind the scenes, rallying support for legislative positions. After leaving the Congress because of eye trouble in 1949, Dirksen found his health restored and launched a successful bid to unseat the Senate Majority Leader, Scott Lucas, in November of 1950. Once again his path crossed that of Richard Nixon who was also elected to the Senate in 1950. Dirksen supported Taft in 1952, giving his nominating speech at the Republican National Convention and providing an emotional highlight of the convention with his dramatic attack on Thomas E. Dewey. Nixon was an Eisenhower supporter, of course, but their close relationship continued and grew as Nixon became the Senate's chief presiding officer in 1953 and Dirksen became an increasingly powerful figure in that body. Both Eisenhower and Nixon welcomed Dirksen's promotion from Whip to Minority Leader in 1959; Eisenhower, in fact, said that for the first time he found his meetings with the congressional leadership enjoyable. And as Nixon began to plan his 1960 presidential campaign he found Dirksen a helpful ally.

Dirksen's ability to rally support for the programs of a Republican President in 1959 and 1960 had been sharply observed by Eisenhower's Democratic successors, John F. Kennedy and Lyndon B. Johnson. Both ardently wooed Dirksen, who consequently emerged during their presidencies as the most powerful Republican in Washington. His support for the United Nations bond issue in 1962, the Nuclear Test Ban Treaty in 1963 and the Civil Rights Act of 1964 all represented reversals of sorts from earlier Dirksen positions, but

37

< *Four Great Americans* >

all were greeted as hallmarks of bipartisan statesmanship. At the same time, the Illinois Senator continued his crusade for many conservative causes, including constitutional amendments to reverse Supreme Court decisions in the fields of school prayer and reapportionment. He also continued to develop his florid oratorical style—which sometimes seemed to poke gentle fun at the pretensions of politicians. Whenever he rose to speak in the Senate, the cry "Ev's up!" would ring through the corridors of the Capitol and reporters would come running from all directions to observe this unique phenomenon.

Re-elected to the Senate in 1956, 1962 and 1968, Dirksen gave the nominating speech for Senator Goldwater at the 1964 Republican Convention and served as Platform Chairman at the convention of 1968. After President Nixon's election, his role changed somewhat—he was no longer the leader of the loyal opposition but rather the President's chief legislative spokesman. Still, he insisted on preserving a certain degree of independence—especially in reacting to potential Administration appointments.

Dirksen served in the Congress under six Presidents and was the Republican Senate Leader under four of them. As President Nixon thought about Dirksen's place in American history, he quickly concluded that each of these Presidents would probably have commented first on Dirksen's unabashed love for the political game and his incomparable skill in playing it. "Ev was a politician and proud of it—he never shied away from that word," the President told an aide as he worked on his speech. "I want to show how he gave luster to the word 'politician.'" It was a natural approach for a man

< *Everett Dirksen* >

whose political career had been so intertwined with Dirksen's and who, like Dirksen, was often criticized as the practitioner of "the old politics" at a time when something called "the new politics"—with its strong emphasis on media and its lessened concern for party organization—was so much in vogue. In a sense, President Nixon's tribute to Everett Dirksen became a tribute to the best elements of "the old politics."

Of course, the eulogy would also have to contain some reference to Senator Dirksen's beloved marigolds. Only a few months earlier, after all, in the middle of a tribute to President Nixon's first sixty days, Dirksen had typically stopped to talk about his flower garden. As for a conclusion, why not the words from Sophocles which President de Gaulle had quoted during his visit to Washington in April of 1960: "One must wait until the evening to see how splendid the day has been." Nixon had been impressed by the thought; he had used it as the conclusion to his memoirs, *Six Crises*, in 1961, and would use it again on other occasions. And in this case it seemed particularly appropriate.

And so on Tuesday, September 9, 1969, for the second time in less than six months, the President of the United States stepped to the rostrum in the Rotunda of the United States Capitol and delivered a solemn but affectionate tribute to an old comrade.   L. W. H.

EULOGY

DELIVERED BY THE PRESIDENT

AT THE GREENWOOD CEMETERY

MARCH 17, 1971

Mrs. YOUNG, friends of Whitney Young:
It is customary on such an occasion for the one who
has the honor to deliver the eulogy to say that we are
gathered here to pay our last respects to the deceased.

I do not say that today. I say, rather, that today a
grateful nation will pay its respect to Whitney Young
by continuing the work for which he dedicated his
entire life.

When we consider that life, these are some of the
things we find:

In an age when we see so many people who want to
be for the right thing, we also find that it is very difficult to accomplish the right thing. It is really easy to be
for what is right. What is more difficult is to accomplish what is right.

< *Four Great Americans* >

And Whitney Young's genius was: He knew how to accomplish what other people were merely for. He was a very complex man, and he understood the complexities of the society in which he lived and the goals which he sought to achieve. He was not a patient man, but he understood the uses of patience.

And he was not a moderate man in terms of his goals, but he knew the uses of moderation in achieving those goals.

All of us who have heard him speak recognize him as one of the most eloquent speakers of our time and, yet, Whitney Young will be remembered as a doer, not a talker.

What monument do we build to him? He leaves his own monument, not one, but thousands, thousands of men and women in his own race who have a chance, an equal chance, that they otherwise might never have had except for what he did; and thousands of others not of his own race who have an understanding in their hearts which they would not have had except for what he taught.

What message does he leave for us? I recall the conversation I had with him right after the election of 1968 before the Inauguration when we discussed the possibilities of his becoming a member of the Cabinet. He

< *Whitney Young* >

was honored by the suggestion and, after consideration, he told me that he felt that he could do more for those things he believed in outside of government than inside of government.

And in that is a message for all of us. At a time when it is so often the custom whenever we have a problem to throw up our hands and say, "What is the government going to do?" this man said, "What can I do?" And that's the challenge he gives to each of us.

Government has its responsibilities, but he says, "What can I do? What can I do in my life to make the American dream come true?" Because all of us must remember we want the American dream to come true, but the American dream cannot come true until the American dream can be achieved by each one who is an American.

Dr. Lon Fuller, in lecturing at Yale in 1963, spoke of two kinds of morality. He spoke of the morality of duty and of the morality of aspiration. The morality of duty is one that requires every individual to do what the law calls upon him to do. The morality of aspiration does not require, but it inspires a man or a woman to go beyond that and to do what the better angels of his nature would call upon him to do.

And it is in that spirit that I speak of Whitney Young

< *Four Great Americans* >

today. I remember the last meeting we had in the Cabinet Room three days before Christmas. You remember, all of you who knew him, he always had a little button, "Equal," in his lapel. He just didn't wear that in his lapel; he wore it in his heart.

And what he says to us and what his message to us is, is this: Every man and woman in this country is equal before God, and every man and woman in this country now, we trust, is equal before the law.

But to have true equality, it is not just what the law requires, but what we individually can do, because that respect which can only come from the heart of one person to another, a respect for his dignity, for his individuality, for his immortality, that is something that must come from each of us.

And so today Whitney Young's message to America—the country that he loved with all of its faults, loved it because he realized that this was a country in which we had the power to change what was wrong and change it peacefully—Whitney Young's message is this: "What can I do? What can I do to make this a better country? What can I do through helping others, through recognizing their equality, their dignity, their individuality, to realize the American dream?"

His dream, if I may paraphrase, was one Nation,

< *Whitney Young* >

under God, indivisible, with liberty and justice and opportunity for all. To fulfill his dream is the responsibility of each of us. It is the commitment that each of us makes in his heart on this day.

———

PRESIDENT NIXON learned of the sudden death of Whitney Young, Jr., in Lagos, Nigeria, while he was in a helicopter en route from the White House to Williamsburg, Virginia, to address the National Conference on the Judiciary on Thursday, March 11, 1971. On arrival at Williamsburg, the report which had been flashed to the helicopter was confirmed for him by an aide, Steven Bull.

The Executive Director of the National Urban League had arrived in Lagos on March 6 for a meeting of the African-American Association. He died while swimming at a popular Lagos bathing area called Lighthouse Beach, apparently of a heart attack. "This is great," he had shouted from the surf. They were his last words. He was only forty-nine years old.

The President promptly directed that a special aircraft from Andrews Air Force Base be dispatched to return Young's body to the United States. And he immediately issued a seven-paragraph statement which began with these words: "With Whitney Young's tragic death today in Nigeria, I have lost a friend—black America has lost a gifted and commanding champion of its just cause—and this nation has lost one of the most compassionate and principled leaders it has had in all the long centuries since whites from Europe and blacks from

45

< *Four Great Americans* >

Africa began building together toward the American dream."

On Friday, March 12, the President traveled to Newport, Rhode Island, to address David Eisenhower's graduating class at the Naval Officer Candidate School. He then headed for his home at Key Biscayne. Meanwhile, in thinking about Young's death and about the significance of his life, the President had decided that he would like to deliver the eulogy if the family would like to have him do so. Aides contacted the family, and found that they would. It was from Florida that the announcement was made on Saturday, March 13, that the President would speak at the burial service for Mr. Young the following Wednesday in Lexington, Kentucky.

The plane bearing Young's body arrived in New York City very late on Sunday afternoon, March 14. Young's widow met the plane at Kennedy Airport and immediately went aboard, standing silently with bowed head before her husband's casket. On Monday and early Tuesday the body lay in state in New York's Riverside Church, where funeral services were held Tuesday morning. The President canceled his Cabinet meeting in Washington so that members could attend the funeral.

The President worked on his eulogy during the weekend in Florida and again on the plane as he returned to Washington on Tuesday, March 16, which was a day of profoundly mixed emotions for the Nixon family. It was not only the day before Young's funeral, but also the day that Thomas E. Dewey —who was to have been a guest at the White House that evening—died suddenly after playing golf in Florida. At the White House that night, with Prime Minister and Mrs. Lynch of Ireland as special guests, the Nixons marked the eve of St.

46

< Whitney Young >

Patrick's Day and Mrs. Nixon's birthday, and announced the engagement of their daughter Tricia to Edward Cox.

Early Wednesday morning, the presidential party left Washington for Lexington, Kentucky. At about the same time, the funeral procession began its eighty-mile journey from Louisville, where Young's body had been brought Tuesday evening, stopping briefly along the way in Lincoln Ridge —the town in which Young was born—and in Frankfort at the Kentucky State College where he went to school.

The two groups met at the Greenwood Cemetery, an old Negro burial ground, parts of which had been overgrown with weeds and strewn with debris only days before. A plot had been made available in a newer cemetery, but Young's family decided he should be buried next to his mother, as had been her wish, and the small and crumbling burial ground had quickly been cleaned and mowed and put in order.

It was a cold, gray day, but despite temperatures in the low thirties, about four thousand persons thronged the cemetery. Many of them had been there since the early morning.

As the President arrived, he placed a wreath of red and white carnations at the graveside, stood at attention with his eyes closed, then sat down next to Mrs. Young. Television cameras allowed the nation to share in the ceremony. As the President spoke, the clouds moved from in front of the sun and he ended his eulogy standing in bright sunlight.

In preparing his farewell, the President was fully aware of the need for brevity. He put together a full written text so that he might achieve the most meaning in the least language, but he did not use the text in Lexington. Deeply moved by the occasion and impressed by its simplicity, he decided to

< *Four Great Americans* >

speak extemporaneously and from the heart, drawing on the ideas he had prepared, to be sure, but also drawing on the inspiration of the moment.

The President had last seen Whitney Young, Jr., on February 24, when he attended a briefing on the President's new domestic policy. But as he prepared his eulogy, the meeting the President remembered most vividly was one held on December 22, 1971, when Young had forcefully presented his suggestions on how the government could work with the Urban League in opening new opportunities for black Americans. As the President noted in his eulogy, Young had come to the meeting with both a sense of crisis and a sense of opportunity.

In briefing the White House press corps after that meeting, Young had emphasized the President's "real concern" for following up on their discussions. After ordering the federal departments to work with the Urban League, the President had asked Young to report back to him on their progress. "Whitney, you call me next month," he had urged the civil-rights leader. Young told the White House reporters of his hope that the meeting would signify ". . . a new start, a new day . . . co-operation of an unprecedented nature." As far as he was concerned, the President "grabbed the ball and ran with it." And he happily recalled that the President had ended the meeting by saying: "What is good for the Urban League is good for the country."

The President's reaction to the meeting had been as enthusiastic as Young's. The Urban League director was "eloquent, tough, and convincing," the President recalled. Of course he had known about these qualities for some time. In

< *Whitney Young* >

1968, just after his election, he had offered Young a Cabinet post in the new Administration. Young declined on the grounds that he could accomplish more outside the government than he could inside the government. The President's eulogy in Lexington would be the first public acknowledgment of the Cabinet discussion.

Whitney Young had begun his work in race relations when he was in the Army. He took an M.A. in social work at the University of Minnesota in 1947 and had worked for the Urban League in St. Paul and Omaha before becoming Dean of the School of Social Work at Atlanta University in 1954. Seven years later he became the Executive Director of the National Urban League. During his ten years in that position he acquired for himself and for his organization a growing reputation for effectiveness in opening economic opportunities for black Americans.

Throughout his career Young had faced one overpowering dilemma: to the degree that he was able to be an effective "Mr. Inside," paving the way for his people by dealing with the leaders of a white power structure, he was to that same degree vulnerable to criticism from more militant blacks who felt that he had sold out to white society. The President was acutely aware of this dilemma—and Young's response to it—as he prepared his remarks. The thing that had always impressed him most about Young was the fact that he did not allow the expectations of others, white or black, to swerve him from the course he thought best for his people.

The test, as Young had put it, was not one of "militant versus moderate, but of responsibility versus irresponsibility, effectiveness versus ineffectiveness." "I am denied the luxury

< *Four Great Americans* >

of rhetoric and one-night stands," he had said. "We stay in town. It calls for a different kind of skill." A highly practical, result-oriented man himself, the President had an immense appreciation for a man who could keep his eye on the ultimate goal and let the chips of popular acclaim or factional approval fall where they may.

Young's goal was what he called "green power." "Pride and dignity," he said, "come when you reach into your pocket and find money, not a hole." This, too, was a philosophy shared by President Nixon, who believed deeply in giving those who bore the special burdens of discrimination a special opportunity to gain "a piece of the action." His efforts to promote "black capitalism" and to advance job opportunity for blacks through efforts such as the Philadelphia Plan were expressions of this commitment.

"What monument do we build to him?" the President asked in his eulogy to Whitney Young, Jr. And he answered by talking of the thousands who now had a chance that they might not otherwise have had. It was a sentiment very close to Young's own answer when asked about his accomplishments. "I tell people," he said, "I can't guarantee you a monument in stone. Your monument will be people helped in moments of distress, people given hope when they had every chance to feel despair. I am not anxious to be the loudest voice, or the most popular. But I would like to think that, at a crucial moment, I was an effective voice of the voiceless, an effective hope for the hopeless."

In President Nixon's view, Young had more than fulfilled that ambition. He was an effective voice of the voiceless, an *effective* hope of the hopeless—with emphasis on the word

< *Whitney Young* >

"effective." It was this sentiment above all else that the President sought to communicate in his eulogy.

A week after the burial, Secretary of Labor James Hodgson appeared at the White House with Whitney Young, Sr., father of the deceased leader, to announce the funding of a new skill center in Kentucky which would be named after Whitney Young, Jr. The center would be located in the old Lincoln Institute, where Whitney Young, Sr., had once been a student, a teacher and president, and where Whitney Young, Jr., had gone to school. In June of 1972, Julie Nixon Eisenhower went to Simpsonville to dedicate the facility.

L. W. H.

EULOGY

DELIVERED BY THE PRESIDENT

AT THE NATIONAL PRESBYTERIAN CHURCH

MAY 4, 1972

D R. ELSON, MRS. EISENHOWER, Your
Excellencies from the Diplomatic Corps, my fellow
Americans:

Today is a day of sadness for America, but it is also
a day of pride. America's pride has always been its
people, a people of good men and women by the millions, of great men and women in remarkable numbers,
and, once in a long while, of giants who stand head and
shoulders above their countrymen, setting a high and
noble standard for us all.

J. Edgar Hoover was one of the giants. His long life
brimmed over with magnificent achievement and dedicated service to this country which he loved so well.
One of the tragedies of life is that, as a rule, a man's
true greatness is recognized only in death. J. Edgar
Hoover was one of the rare exceptions to that rule.
He became a living legend while still a young man,

53

< *Four Great Americans* >

and he lived up to his legend as the decades passed. His death only heightens the respect and admiration felt for him across this land and in every land where men cherish freedom.

The greatness of Edgar Hoover will remain inseparable from the greatness of the organization he created and gave his whole life to building, the Federal Bureau of Investigation. He made the FBI the finest law enforcement agency on the earth, the invincible and incorruptible defender of every American's precious right to be free from fear.

Yet, America has revered this man not only as the Director of an institution but as an institution in his own right. For nearly half a century, nearly one fourth of the whole history of this Republic, J. Edgar Hoover has exerted a great influence for good in our national life. While eight Presidents came and went, while other leaders of morals and manners and opinion rose and fell, the Director stayed at his post.

I recall that President Eisenhower, a Republican, and President Johnson, a Democrat, both strongly recommended, after my election, that I keep him as Director of the FBI. He was one of those unique individuals who, by all odds, was the best man for a vitally important job. His powerful leadership by example

< *J. Edgar Hoover* >

helped to keep steel in America's backbone and the flame of freedom in America's soul.

He personified integrity; he personified honor; he personified principle; he personified courage; he personified discipline; he personified dedication; he personified loyalty; he personified patriotism. These are his legacies to the Bureau he built and the nation he served. We can pay him no higher tribute than to live these virtues ourselves, as he lived them all of his years, to love the law as he loved it, and to give fullest respect, support and co-operation to the law enforcement profession which he did so much to advance.

When such a towering figure—a man who has dominated his field so completely for so many years —finally passes from the scene, there is sometimes a tendency to say, "Well, this is an end of an era."

There is a belief that a changing of the guard will also mean a changing of the rules. With J. Edgar Hoover this will not happen. The FBI will carry on in the future, true to its finest traditions in the past, because regardless of what the snipers and detractors would have us believe, the fact is that Director Hoover built the Bureau totally on principle, not on personality. He built well. He built to last. For that reason, the FBI will remain as a memorial to him, a living

< *Four Great Americans* >

memorial, continuing to create a climate of protection, security and impartial justice that benefits every American.

The good J. Edgar Hoover has done will not die. The profound principles associated with his name will not fade away. Rather, I would predict that in the time ahead those principles of respect for law, order and justice will come to govern our national life more completely than ever before. Because the trend of permissiveness in this country, a trend which Edgar Hoover fought against all his life, a trend which was dangerously eroding our national heritage as a law-abiding people, is now being reversed.

The American people today are tired of disorder, disruption and disrespect for law. America wants to come back to the law as a way of life, and as we do come back to the law, the memory of this great man, who never left the law as a way of life, will be accorded even more honor than it commands today.

In times past, in the days of the American frontier, the brave men who wore the badge and enforced the law were called by a name we do not often hear today. They were called "peace officers." Today, though that term has passed out of style, the truth it expressed still endures. All the world yearns for peace, peace among

< *J. Edgar Hoover* >

nations, peace within nations. But without peace officers, we can never have peace. Edgar Hoover knew this basic truth. He shaped his life around it. He was the peace officer without peer.

The United States is a better country because this good man lived his long life among us these past seventy-seven years. Each of us stands forever in his debt. In the years ahead, let us cherish his memory. Let us be true to his legacy. Let us honor him as he would surely want us to do, by honoring all the men and women who carry on in this noble profession of helping to keep the peace in our society.

In the Bible, the book which Edgar Hoover called his "guide to daily life," we find the words which best pronounce a benediction on his death. They are from the Psalms: "Great peace have they which love Thy law." J. Edgar Hoover loved the law of his God. He loved the law of his country. And he richly earned peace through all eternity.

J. EDGAR HOOVER was born on New Year's Day in 1895 in southeast Washington, D.C., and he lived all his life in the nation's capital. He attended Central High School, became a cataloguer in the Library of Congress, earned a law degree at night from George Washington University and at the age of twenty-two went to work in the Justice Department's Enemy Alien Registration Section. Seven years later, Attorney General Harlan Fisk Stone appointed the twenty-nine-year-old Hoover as Director of the Department's Bureau of Investigation, instructing him to repair its reputation for corruption and inefficiency. Hoover soon accomplished that goal—and he never left the position.

The FBI's effective crusade against crime and communism made Hoover a national hero in the 1930s, 1940s and 1950s, a figure of legendary proportions even while still a young man. In later years, however, he became an increasingly controversial figure, and the controversy reached a peak after President Nixon took office. On every hand there were cries for Hoover's scalp. Some of the President's advisers even suggested that perhaps Hoover should be asked to leave in order to quiet the critics. But Richard Nixon would not hear of it. Whatever the public clamor, he felt the Director deserved his loyalty. He never wavered in his support.

Though Hoover was seventy-seven years old, his death still came as a profound shock to the country and to its President. Physically and spiritually, his image had been that of an indestructible man. His health had been excellent. He had worked a full day on Monday, May 1, 1972, leaving his office at 5 P.M. He had dined at the home of his close friend, Associate FBI Director Clyde A. Tolson, and had retired to his home at the edge of Washington's Rock Creek Park where he lived alone. When he failed to appear as usual the next morning, his housekeeper, Annie Fields, went to his room and found his body lying beside the bed. Doctors said he died during the night of hypertensive cardiovascular disease.

< J. Edgar Hoover >

The President learned of Hoover's death from his assistant, H. R. Haldeman, who went into the President's office with the news immediately on being informed of it in a telephone call from Acting Attorney General Richard Kleindienst. No public statement was made, however, until the news had been flashed to FBI offices across the country. At 11 o'clock a formal public announcement was issued by Mr. Kleindienst and, at 11:10 A.M., President Nixon stepped before the cameras in the briefing room at the White House to make a personal comment to the American people.

"It is with a profound sense of personal loss," he began, "that I learned of the death of J. Edgar Hoover." He remarked on Hoover's "unparalleled devotion and ability and dedication" and observed that Hoover "for twenty-five years, from the time I came to Washington as a freshman Congressman, has been one of my closest personal friends and advisers." The President acknowledged the "sometimes very vicious attack" to which Hoover had been subjected. And, referring to his order that all flags over government buildings be flown at half mast, he concluded by saying that Hoover "made certain that the flag of the FBI will always fly high."

The President turned next to two tasks—preparing a eulogy for Hoover's funeral on Thursday morning and selecting the Director's successor. By the next day, he had determined that L. Patrick Gray III should serve as Acting Director of the FBI until a permanent nomination could be considered by the Senate without its being embroiled in the pressure of election-year politics. Mr. Gray's designation was announced to the press at 3:40 P.M. on Wednesday, May 3.

As for the eulogy, the President did some preliminary work

< *Four Great Americans* >

on Tuesday afternoon and evening and then completed the task late on Wednesday afternoon. He decided immediately that he wanted to use this occasion to honor not only Hoover himself but also the great values for which Hoover stood: national respect for the rule of law and for those who devote their lives to enforcing it.

The President felt he did not need to go through a long list of Hoover's achievements. The Director's record was well known and could speak for itself. One of the tragedies of life, the President remarked as he worked on the speech, is that a person's accomplishments are often unrecognized until after his death. But in this case it was different. And so the eulogy could focus on those elements in Hoover's character which both represented and inspired the American people.

The President deeply admired the way Hoover had persevered in the face of intense criticism. He wryly observed that many of those who were now lavishly praising the dead Director had been among his most virulent opponents. And when an aide remarked that the President's language would set him clearly among the ranks of Hoover's most ardent admirers, the President responded—quickly and emphatically: "That's where I've always been."

Immediately after learning of Hoover's death, the Congress had passed a special resolution making it possible for his body to lie in state in the Capitol Rotunda, the first time this honor had been accorded a civil servant. Chief Justice Warren Burger delivered a brief eulogy there at noon on Wednesday, May 3, and then, despite a pouring rain, visitors arrived throughout the day at a rate of about one thousand an hour to pay their final respects. At midnight they were still com-

< *J. Edgar Hoover* >

ing, though the Capitol steps by then had been taken over by a candlelight vigil protesting the Vietnam war.

On Thursday morning Hoover's body was moved to the National Presbyterian Church in northwest Washington. Hoover, who had considered becoming a minister while a young man, had been an active member of the church all his life. As a boy he had sung in its choir and twice he had served as a trustee. He was a close friend of Dr. L. R. Elson, pastor of the church and chaplain of the Senate, who visited Hoover each year on January 1, his birthday. Elson had also been President Eisenhower's minister and had, in fact, baptized the late President in 1953.

Over two thousand invited guests filled the sanctuary of the modernistic white stone church on Nebraska Avenue. The building was less than three years old. In fact, the first funeral ever held in the church had been the funeral service in September 1969 for Everett McKinley Dirksen. The President and Mrs. Nixon arrived at 10:30 A.M., accompanied by the new Acting Director of the FBI and Mrs. Gray, and were seated next to Mamie Eisenhower.

After Dr. Elson's remarks, the Lord's Prayer, the singing of two hymns by the Army chorus, the reading of Psalms and New Testament passages, President Nixon moved to the lectern and delivered his eulogy. Once again the nation shared in the solemn moment through television and radio. At the conclusion of his remarks, the President stood silently for a moment before the coffin with Dr. Elson, then returned to his pew for the benediction.

The Director was buried next to his parents in Washington's Congressional Cemetery—a site just thirteen blocks

< *Four Great Americans* >

from the row house where he had been born in 1895. The flag from the coffin was presented to Clyde Tolson.

The President said in his eulogy that the FBI would always be Hoover's "living memorial." As a concrete symbol of this fact, the President, upon returning to the White House that day, designated the new FBI Building, then under construction in Washington, as the J. Edgar Hoover Building.

L. W. H.